# SCRIABIN

## SELECTED WORKS FOR THE PIANO

### EDITED BY MURRAY BAYLOR

## AN ALFRED MASTERWORK EDITION

Second Edition
Copyright © MMII by Alfred Publishing Co., Inc.
All rights reserved. Printed in USA.
ISBN 0-7390-3190-2

*Cover art:* Interior with piano
   *by Fernand Lantoine (1876–1936)*
   *Waterhouse and Dodd, London, Great Britain*
   *Fine Art Photographic Library, London/Art Resource, New York*

# ALEXANDER SCRIABIN*

Born, Moscow, January 6, 1872 (Christmas, 1871,
according to the old Russian calendar)
Died, Moscow, April 14, 1915 (Easter, according
to the old Russian calendar)

Scriabin is often, with justice, called a "piano composer." When he died at the age of 43 he had composed in 32 years almost 200 pieces, large and small, for solo piano. Aside from a few immature attempts at song and chamber music, six large works for orchestra, and one for piano and orchestra, his piano solo music constitutes his oeuvre. Like Chopin, he played the piano extremely well, loved the sound of it, and wrote most easily and idiomatically for his favorite instrument. His music is controversial today and it was in Scriabin's time, as one can see in these excerpts from two reviews:

The nerves of the audience were worn and racked as nerves are seldom assailed even these days. Scriabin's *Poème de l'ecstase* was the cause . . . . Most of the time the violins were whimpering and wailing like lost souls, while strange undulating and formless melodies roved about in the woodwind. A solo violin spoke occasionally, growing more and more plaintive, and finally getting swallowed up in a chaos of acid harmonies with violins screaming in agony overhead. There were three such climaxes in the composition, all built upon the basis of cymbals, drums and inchoate blarings of the brass. It all seemed far more like several other things than ecstasy.

W.J. Henderson, New York Sun,
December 11, 1908

Some of the ecstasy was extremely bitter, while some of it reminded one of the ecstasy of the two convivial gentlemen who thought that the air was filled with green monkeys with crimson eyes and sparkling tails, a kind of ecstasy that is sold in Russia at two rubles a bottle.

Louis Elson, Boston Daily Advertiser,
October 2, 1910

---

* The name of the composer has been variously transliterated from the Cyrillic alphabet. In our alphabet one may find the name spelled Scriabine, Skriabin, Skryabin, or Skrjabine, as well as in the most common spelling given above. Russians pronounce the name "Skree-*ah*-bean," accenting the middle syllable.

On the other hand, a short time later Ernest Newman, a distinguished, respected English music critic, found that the music expressed for him "the soul of man slowly yearning into conscious being out of a primal undifferentiated world, torn by the conflict of emotions, violently purging itself of grossness, and ultimately winning its way to light." "The wind that blows through the music," he continued, "is the veritable wind of the cosmos itself. Listening to it solely as music, only a congenitally unimaginative dullard, or a musician sodden with the futile teaching of the textbooks and the conservatories, could not help feeling that here is music that comes as near as is at present possible to being the pure voice of Nature and the soul themselves." Dr. Eaglefield Hull, another distinguished critic and musical scholar, thought the piano sonatas of Scriabin destined to occupy a niche of their own, together with the 48 preludes and fugues of Bach, the 32 sonatas of Beethoven, and the piano music of Chopin.

## The Man

Like most other very gifted musicians, Scriabin showed outstanding musical ability as a child and was unusually sensitive to musical sounds. He had synesthesia (sensations of seeing color when he heard musical pitches), and he consistently related certain pitches to certain colors. After some early piano instruction with his aunt and a private teacher, he entered the Moscow Conservatory at the age of 16, where Serge Rachmaninoff, one year his junior, was a fellow student. He graduated from the conservatory with a diploma and a gold medal in piano, but with no similar recognition in composition because of a personality conflict with A. Arensky, his composition teacher. Soon after graduation he was befriended by M.P. Belaieff, a music publisher who gave him financial subsidy, arranged concert tours largely devoted to his own music, in Germany, France, Holland, and Belgium, and published his music almost as soon as each new work was written. For five years he taught piano at the Moscow Conservatory, but when a wealthy merchant who had once been his student offered him an annuity to allow him more time for composition he accepted and went to Switzerland where he lived for most of two years.

He married Vera Isakovitch, a fine pianist, who did a great deal to make his music known to concertgoers, but in 1905, when he went to Paris for the premiere of his *Divine Poem*, they separated. He had fallen in love with Tatiana Schloezer, the sister of a Russian music critic, who had admired him for years. She became his new inspiration and companion. In Brussels, where he lived for two years, he became acquainted with a Mme. H.P. Blavatsky and renewed contact

4

with mystical ideas that had first intrigued him in Russia through conversations with friends and his reading of some of the great Russian poets and novelists. Some of these religious and philosophic ideas, later to be known as Theosophy, were concerned with intuitive insight on the part of certain individuals who held that there is a divinity to nature, which is manifested in the universe. Scriabin became more and more deeply influenced by these ideas, as the titles and programs of his later works indicate; his last works for orchestra might be called philosophical program music, and many of his "Poems" for piano are the equivalent of orchestral tone poems. He had always been interested in colors as they related to music in his hypersensitive consciousness, and for his *Prometheus* or *Poem of Fire,* Op. 60, first conducted by Koussevitsky in 1908, he prepared a part for a color keyboard, the invention of an Englishman named Rimington, which projected colored light on a screen while the music was being played. For practical reasons, the color accompaniment had to be omitted from the first performance. The work was performed only once with the color projections, at a concert in 1914 in New York, apparently with disappointing effect. Scriabin's successful concert tour of the United States was cut short when his mistress joined him in New York and a scandal ensued. There was the strong possibility that they might be deported for "moral turpitude," so they hastily sailed for Europe where the climate was less puritanical.

At the end of his life Scriabin was planning a gigantic new work, a *Mystery* which was to involve music, poetry, acting, dance (compare L. Bernstein's recent *Mass*), projected colors, and perfumes created by incense. He conceived this work not simply as a feast for all the senses, but as a kind of festival in which people from many parts of the world would take part, and which would express the unity of mankind with the Divine Being. Scriabin saw himself by this time not only as a creative artist but as a kind of prophet or redeemer doing a great good for the world by giving the participants in the work (they were to be more than audience) new insights into higher spiritual planes. The work was barely begun, with some preliminary sketches on paper, when the composer had a recurrence of a boil on his upper lip and died of blood poisoning. As a footnote to this account of Scriabin's life, Boris Pasternak, author of *Doctor Zhivago,* took piano lessons from Scriabin when he was a child and wrote about their acquaintance. Scriabin's only living descendant, a daughter, Marina Scriabin, now lives in Paris.

# The Music

Scriabin's music has always been difficult for scholars to "place" in the history of music. It shows no influence of the music of the Russian nationalists who were around Scriabin as he was maturing. He had no strong continuing influence on later composers, starting no "school." Yet he was the precursor of many trends in twentieth-century music—chord clusters, additive melodic fragmentation, serialism, and the psychedelic combination of sounds and colors now called "mixed media." Since he firmly believed that music has a consciousness-expanding effect on the listener, his music and the ideas behind his music have intrigued many people since the mid-1960s. Few listeners fail to respond to the emotional power or the rich sound combinations of most of Scriabin's music.

As a young man Scriabin admired, most of all, the music of Chopin and as a young composer, modeled his own music consciously or unconsciously on that of his idol. Although this early music has considerable individuality, it reminds us of Chopin, not only because he used the same generic titles (prelude, waltz, mazurka, etude, impromptu, nocturne, etc.), but also because of the idiomatic piano writing, the ingratiating harmony, and the eloquent melodic lines. There are many elegant miniatures from this period, all admirably suited to the medium. Over a period of several years Scriabin, like Chopin, wrote a set of preludes in all the major and minor keys (Op. 11), an idea to be taken up later by Rachmaninoff, Shostakovitch, and Kabalevsky. His etudes, like those of Chopin, explore pianistic difficulties with beautiful sound and distinctive style. The classically parallel phrase structure, the richly colored sonorities and the affecting melody of the Etude in C sharp minor, Op. 2, No. 1, are strongly reminiscent of the Polish master. Somewhat like etudes are the Prelude and Nocturne, Op. 9, for the left hand alone. They were written during a time when the right side of his collar bone was mending from a break suffered in an accident and he was only able to play the piano with his left hand. It might be said in passing that pianists of less than virtuoso left hand technique may enjoy the music by playing it with both hands.

Beginning approximately with Opus 18 one senses the harmonic influence of Liszt and Wagner, with more chromaticism, more seventh chords on the supertonic, and more frequent seventh and ninth chords, some with a diminished or an augmented fifth. The Prelude, Op. 27, No. 1, is notable for its use of the augmented sixth chord, known as the French sixth, and the curiously delayed resolutions of nonchord tones, as well as its masterful layout on the keyboard for powerfully balanced resonance. In this period, in the larger works, Scriabin was starting his experiments with sonata form using the cyclic idea, combining elements of variations with sonata form, combining rondo and variation elements, etc. The fourth sonata, beginning with a languorously reflective introduction, moves to excited agitation, massive climaxes, and an orgiastic coda reminiscent of Liszt. All the sonatas after the fourth are in one movement. The *Poème Satanique*, Op. 36, reminds us of Liszt's diabolism and seems to prefigure Prokofieff's *Suggestion Diabolique* with its evocation of the evil in the world.

There is no Opus 50, but in the music with opus numbers above 50, particularly beginning with the fifth sonata, written in 1907, Scriabin's music reaches a maximum individuality because of compositional techniques he was discovering that link him to later composers. The piece called *Enigma*, Op. 52 suggests Schoenberg's Op. 19 in stretching tonality almost to the vanishing point. Finding superposed triads too restrictive, Scriabin began to build chords in fourths rather than thirds, arbitrarily choosing the more remote and complex relationships of the harmonic series to relate to the root (see examples).

## Harmonic Series

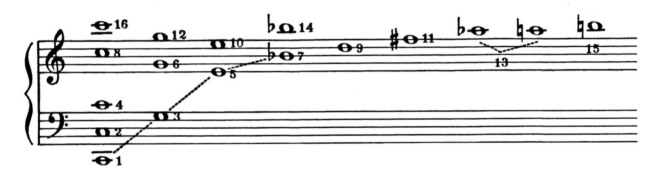

## "Mystic Chord" and Scale Formation

For several works, particularly for *Prometheus*, Op. 60, Scriabin used what has been called his "mystic," or "mystery," chord as the characteristic sonority. The combination of augmented, diminished, and perfect fourths give the chord richness and plasticity. Though it can be inverted and written as a projection of thirds to become a kind of thirteenth chord, the spread, in context, makes it sound like superposed fourths having nothing to do with thirds. It is simplistic to say that this was his main harmonic innovation in the latter part of his life. Almost every new work from this period had a different chord. In the two piano pieces Op. 57, the "key chord" is (reading up from the bass): C, F♯, B, E; in the eighth sonata it is A, D♯, G, C♯, F, B, E. In most of the late works a strange, exotic-sounding chord of this kind becomes the consonance around and through which dissonances move. This results in a blurring of the significant distinction between consonance and dissonance. As before, a chord built a tritone away from the "tonic" becomes the main point of harmonic tension, equivalent to a dominant. In the piece *Désir,* Op. 57, written in 1908, the threshold of atonality and/or polytonality is reached. The effect of languid eroticism is partly a result of the tempo and rhythms, but even more a result of the chord structures. Key signatures disappear after Op. 58, being no longer useful. In all of Scriabin's works of this period one feels less and less effect of harmonic punctuation, as a result of weakened cadential moves. Sometimes different and conflicting rhythmic patterns overlap in a remarkable way.

When they do not, the phraseology is rather simple and straightforward, two- and four-measure units being the rule. After the early works, piano figures were seldom the conventional ones with Scriabin, and now they become still less conventional. Trills, which occur frequently, produce a kind of nervous excitement, as in the morbidly gloomy Ninth Sonata, because of their placement in the texture and their rhythmic function. Melodies continue to move most frequently by upward leaps, so that the overall effect is one of great originality. There is nothing quite like this in music until we come to the works of Olivier Messiaen many years later. The unusual directions to the performer—"with a celestial voluptuousness," "winged," "with an exalted joy," "swirling," etc.—were probably added by or at the suggestion of his mistress. Though they often seem strained or puzzling, they do sometimes suggest an atmosphere to the performer; keeping these indications in mind, he can make the music sound exalted, excited or ecstatic.

All the contemporary accounts of Scriabin's playing of his own music describe his wonderful pedaling, which made the piano seem to overcome its limitations and sing and sustain. Unfortunately he, like Debussy, almost never indicated pedaling. The editor has added suggested pedaling, fingering, and, in a few cases, a less awkward distribution of the notes between the hands.

# Recommended Reading

Bowers, Faubion. *Scriabin: A Biography of the Russian Composer*. Tokyo and Palo Alto: Kodansha International Ltd., 1969.

Bowers, Faubion. *The New Scriabin; Enigma and Answers*. New York: St. Martin's Press, 1973.

Hull, Eaglefield. *Scriabin, a Great Russian Tone Poet*. London: Kegan Paul Trench, Trubner and Co., Ltd., 1927.

Montagu-Nathan, M. *Handbook of the Pianoforte Works of Scriabin*. London: J. and W. Chester, 2nd edition, 1922.

Swan, Alfred J. *Scriabin*. London: The Bodley Head, 1923 and 1928. (Reprinted by Greenwood and also by Da Capo Press.)

# Recommended Recordings

Currently available recordings of Scriabin's piano music include beautiful interpretations of various works by Vladimir Ashkenazy, Morton Estrin, Glenn Gould, Vladimir Horowitz, Anton Kuerti, Ruth Laredo, Victor Merzhanov, Michael Ponti, Sergei Prokofieff, Sergei Rachmaninoff, Sviatoslav Richter, Hans-Helmut Schwartz, Roberto Szidon, Sergei Tarnowsky and Igor Zhukov.

Pianists who appreciate Scriabin's music look forward to the time when the complete edition of his piano music, so well begun by Professors K. Igumnov and J. Milstein for the State Music Publisher of the Soviet Union, will be continued, and when the volumes now out of print will be reprinted.

# Playing Scriabin

To the student approaching Scriabin's music for the first time, the polyrhythms are often a hurdle to be overcome. These can be worked out on graph paper for easy visualization and, when the notes can be played easily hands alone, the passage can be practised slowly hands together with the necessary sub-divisions until it is possible to hear and play the interlocked rhythms at the required speed. The Etude in F minor, Op.42, No. 7, for example, presents the problem of playing eighth note triplets with the right hand while playing groups of four sixteenths with the left, the same problem that Chopin posed in the same key with vastly different effect in one of his etudes. When the student is able to play and hear the combinations of the rhythms as this figure:

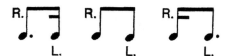

he is ready to move forward into the matters of phrasing, pedaling, expression, etc., which will make the piece come alive as music. Another more complex example of Scriabin's polyrhythms is in the second section of the *Poem,* Op. 32, No. 1 beginning at measure 15. One may diagram this combination of quintuplet and triplet which oc-

curs later in the section as follows:

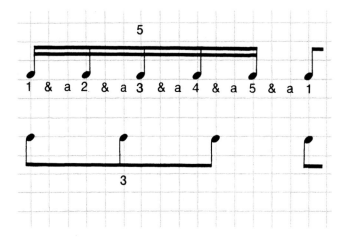

Play the notes of the right hand quintuplet counting 1&a, 2&a, 3&a, 4&a, 5&a while putting the left hand notes into the proper time-slot. When this can be done accurately and easily, only consciously coordinating the hands at the beginning of each beat, it will be possible to shorten the last notes of the rhythmic unit in measure 15 and similar measures to take care of the interpolated rests and the shortened note values found in this variant of the basic pattern.

Another problem in learning this music is the question of which notes to play with which hand, and this is less simple than it appears at first glance. Scriabin often wrote large, resonant chords for both hands in the center of the keyboard with octave doublings and crossed thumbs as in the Etude, Op. 2, No. 1. Other times he wrote in a very wide keyboard range—a high melody, low bass notes sustained by the pedal, and middle harmony filled in by both hands. At times his notation divides the notes to be played between the hands in a convenient and musically effective way, and it is easy to read the notes as they stand and produce the right pitches, in the right time and tempo, with all the appropriate emphasis. At other times, the composer's notation, if taken literally, stretches the hands unmercifully, puts the performer into awkward hand-across-body positions, or requires quick treacherous leaps of the hand which endanger accuracy, balance, or the polish that comes with comparative ease of execution. As one studies the music it becomes apparent that it is notated so that the different musical functions of the note successions are clear to the reader (melody vs. accompaniment, or bass line vs. harmonic upper-structure, for example), and this may have little to do with playing convenience. As with the music of other composers, when lines cross or converge, the intent of the notation is not to direct the pianist to put one finger of each hand on the same key, but to show the shape and continuity of the individual lines so that he understands the music. Since musical notation is descriptive rather than prescriptive, it seems wise to divide the notes to be played between the hands in a way that gives the player maximum security and ease in performance while achieving the intended musical effect. Reading the music with pedantic literalness often produces awkward-sounding, unmusical results. This edition parenthesizes notes to be omitted when lines converge, and suggests a rather large number of hand divisions.

Scriabin wrote for the modern piano as a richly resonant instrument, using the full range of the keyboard and assuming the use of the pedal about ninety percent of the time. Bell-like and harp-like effects are common. Tenor melodies, often played with the left hand thumb, move concurrently with high soprano melodies and lush harmony below and above them. Such effects are only possible with the pedal. Melodies float out from a haze of pedaled chords. Arpeggio formations sweep downward in the left hand to make a kind of crescendo as the pedal piles up resonance to the lowest note. Pedaled repeated notes or chords sometimes become a substitute for the kind of sustained tone that the piano cannot produce. In music of this complexity and subtlety, and with few hints from the composer, it is impossible to give final answers on how the pedaling should be done. Decisions about pedaling depend on: the fingering that is coordinated with the pedaling, the piano, the resonance of the room, the dynamic levels used, the balance of parts, and the skill of the performer. The pedaling given here should serve until the performer discovers a better one for himself.

Trills always start on the principal note. When the upper auxilliary of the trilled note is to be sharped or flatted it is so indicated; otherwise the key signature prevails. Pitches notated in small size notes are always short like *acciacature*. When several of these small notes move upward disjunctly to a higher pitch printed in normal size type they are played like a rolled chord pushing toward the larger top note which has melodic significance. Low bass *acciacature* are played quickly but pedaled before the finger leaves the key in order to sustain the note into the chord which follows, and give support to the upper structure. Very widely spaced chords are sometimes indicated as rolled chords and sometimes not. When they are not so marked they should be rolled nevertheless, but quickly. Staccato marks, as in Chopin, sometimes indicate the kind of touch and resultant tone quality rather than shortened note values, and therefore may be pedaled.

According to the conventions of his time, and according to all contemporary reports, Scriabin played with rubato and assumed it would be used by performers. This does not mean that the music should be played with minimal rhythmic continuity or in some kind of spineless, vague fashion. A steady rhythmic pulse which moves forward with grace and flexibility, and is held back or pushed forward occasionally for expressive purpose is ideal for this music as it is for most late romantic music. The pianist must, in his performance, keep a sense of the phrase lengths and the balance of symmetrical phrases. He should spread the beats appropriately in melodic climaxes, for important bass progressions, for surprising harmonic turns, or similar points of musical interest but not lose a firm grip on the basic pulse. Particularly in the later works when the chord structures retain little feeling of functional harmony it is important that the performer make clear for the listener the complex time relationships and the rhythms of the phrases if the projection of the music is to be beautiful and convincing.

A student starting a new piece might ask himself questions of this kind:

1) What is the all-over form of the piece? If it is ternary, is the return literal, or is it changed? Why?

2) What are the time lengths of the melodic phrases—how many beats or how many measures? Where is the main point of emphasis of each phrase?

3) What do you find about the succession of phrases and their relation to each other? For example—is an opening phrase of four measures balanced by another of equivalent length or by two of half the length as the piece continues? Could two four-measure phrases be followed appropriately by one of eight measures in a quick tempo? If the phrase structure has this kind of symmetry, is it changed or modified as the piece moves forward? How?

4) Are there simultaneous melodic lines? Which one should be highlighted? Or should the highlight shift from one to the other?

5) Where are the most important harmonic shifts or changes of tonal direction in the piece? How are they accomplished? Do they relate to the all-over form of the piece?

6) Is it possible to "block" this piece by playing a condensed harmonic outline of it?

7) Where should the main climax come?

8) What mood or atmosphere should this music create?

9) What are the main technical difficulties? What might be a fruitful way of working on them?

12

Scriabin in 1898.

Scriabin in 1892.

Sketch of Scriabin in 1905, drawn by
Leonid Pasternak, father of Boris.

Scriabin in 1914.

Scriabin and Tatiana with their son Julian in 1913. Julian drowned six years later at the age of 11.

Scriabin's manuscript for *"Desire."*

## Acknowledgments

The editor is indebted to Dr. Wasil G. Fiedorow for bringing photographs of Scriabin's manuscripts from Moscow and to Mme. Tatyana Shaborkina, Director of the Scriabin State Museum.

# Etude in C♯ Minor

Op. 2, No. 1
( 1887 ) *

* The year of the work given is according to a chronological list of his early works made by Scriabin in 1889.

† m.d.—Abbrev. for *mano destra* (Ital.) right hand

   m.s.—Abbrev. for *mano sinistra* (Ital.) left hand

# (a) Prelude in E Minor

Op. 11, No. 4
(1888)

(a) The work was begun in another key-in B flat minor-and was to have been a ballade.

On this fragment Scriabin wrote, "Beautiful country. Life here is different."

(b) This was originally started in 3/4 time but was changed to 6/4 time on the autograph.

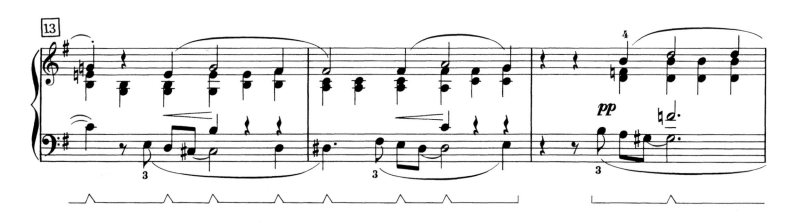

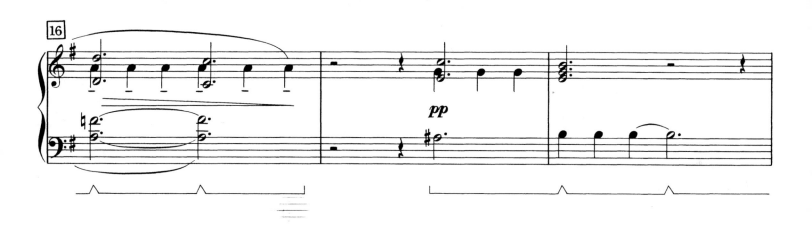

# Prelude in B Minor

Op. 11, No. 6
(1889)

\* or better

# Prelude in G♭

Op. 16, No.3
( 1894 )

(a) Here, in the autograph, 32 measures are scratched out.

# Prelude for Left Hand Alone

Op. 9, No. 1
(1894)

(half Pedal)

# Etude in D♯ Minor

Op. 8, No. 12
( 1894 )

There is an alternate version of this etude which Scriabin never authorized for publication.

(a)  The autograph has an *fp* in the first measure.

30

(a) In the autograph there is a completely different dynamic plan, namely:

# Prelude in A Minor

Op. 11, No. 2
(1895)

(a) Here, according to the composer, a small caesura is possible, followed by **pp**.
(b) The dashes above the notes here are by the composer.

(c) Accel.⁓According to the composer.

(d) ⎱ See footnote (a).
(e) ⎰

# Prelude in C

Op. 11, No. 1
( 1895 )

(a) At first, Scriabin wrote at the beginning of the piece Ondeggiante Carezzando (swaying and caressing),
later removing the first word from the autograph. In correcting proofs he changed Carezzando to Vivace.

34

(b) ♩ in the autograph and Belaieff's edition.

# Prelude in G Minor

Op. 27, No.1
( 1900 )

# Prelude in B

Op. 27, No. 2
( 1900 )

# Etude in F♯

("The Mosquito")

Op. 42, No. 3
(1903)

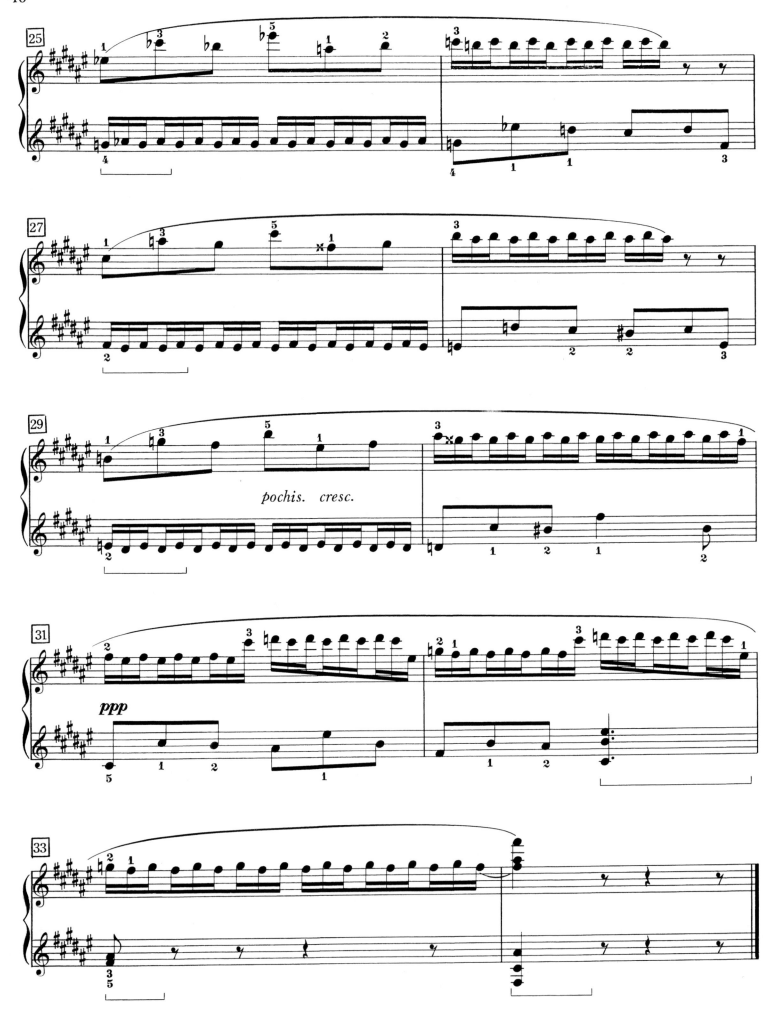

# Etude in F Minor

Op. 42, No. 7
(1903)

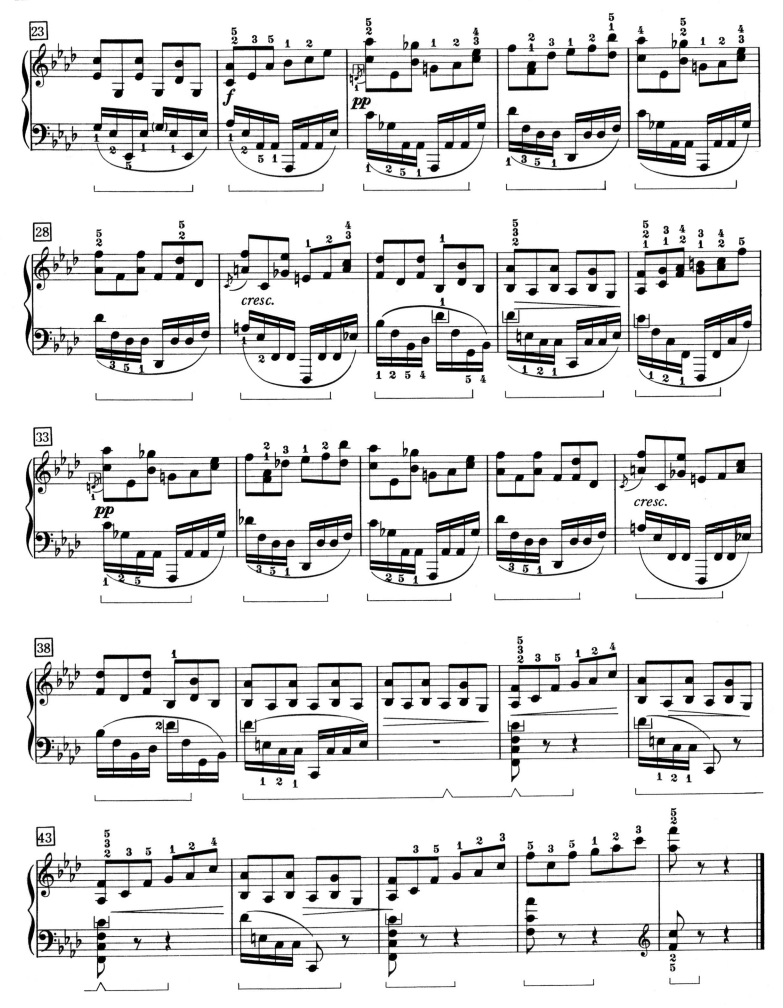

# Poem in F♯

Op. 32, No. 1
(1903)

*inaferando (not hurrying)*

# Poem in D

**Allegro** (with elegance and with confidence) (♩ = 84~88)

Op. 32, No. 2
(1903)

# Mazurka

Op. 40, No. 1
(1903)

51

# Fourth Sonata in F♯

## I

Op. 30
(1903-4)

attacca

# II

**A flying prestissimo** ( ♩. =160)

57

62

The four "Ped" signs in this section appeared in the original edition and, as was usual when Scriabin indicated pedaling, were intended to show exceptions to the common practice of his time.

# Prelude in C

Op. 48, No.2
(1905)

# Quasi Valse

Op. 47
(1906)

# Album Leaf in E♭

Op. 45, No. 1
(1907)

# Winged Poem

Op. 51, No.3
(1907)

# Languorous Dance

Op. 51, No. 4
(1907)

# Ironies

Op. 56, No.2
(1908)

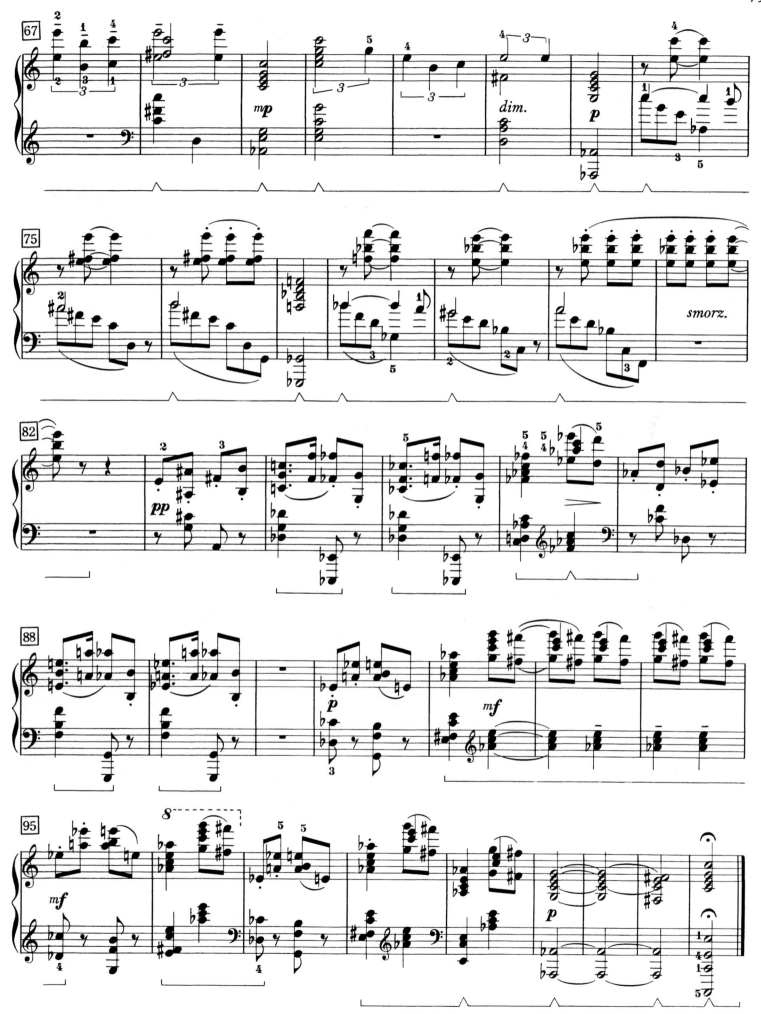

# Nuances

Op. 56, No. 3
(1908)

Molten, velvety ( ♩. = C. 63 )

# Desire

Op. 57
(1908)

# Strangeness

Op. 63, No. 2
(1911 - 12)

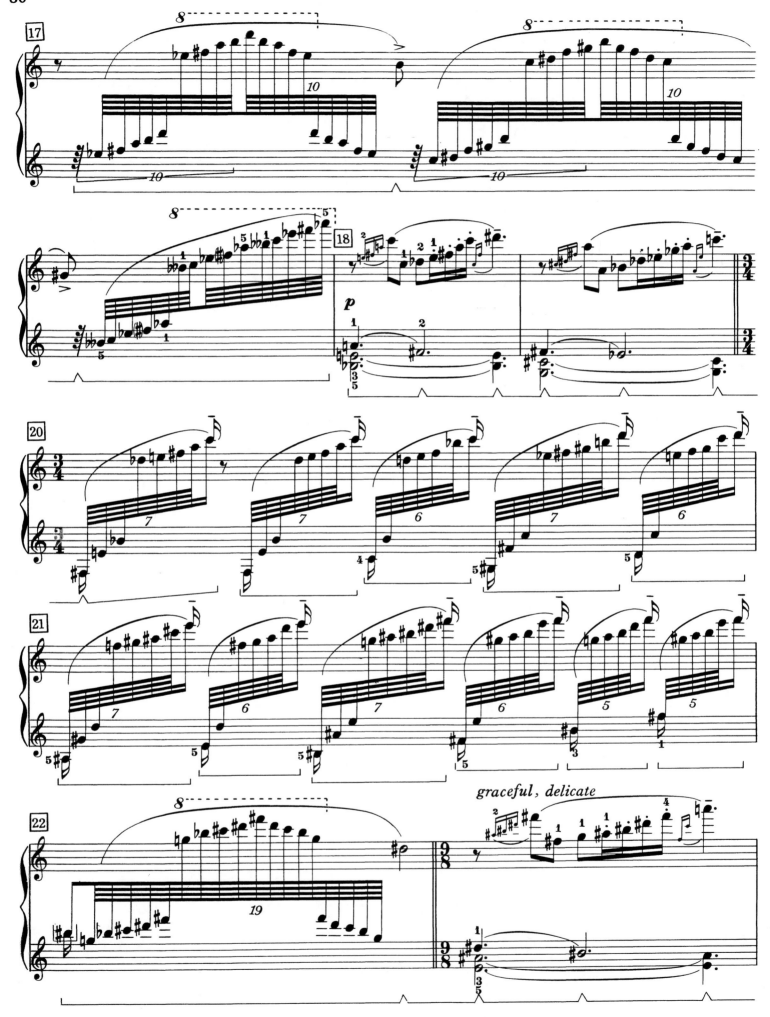

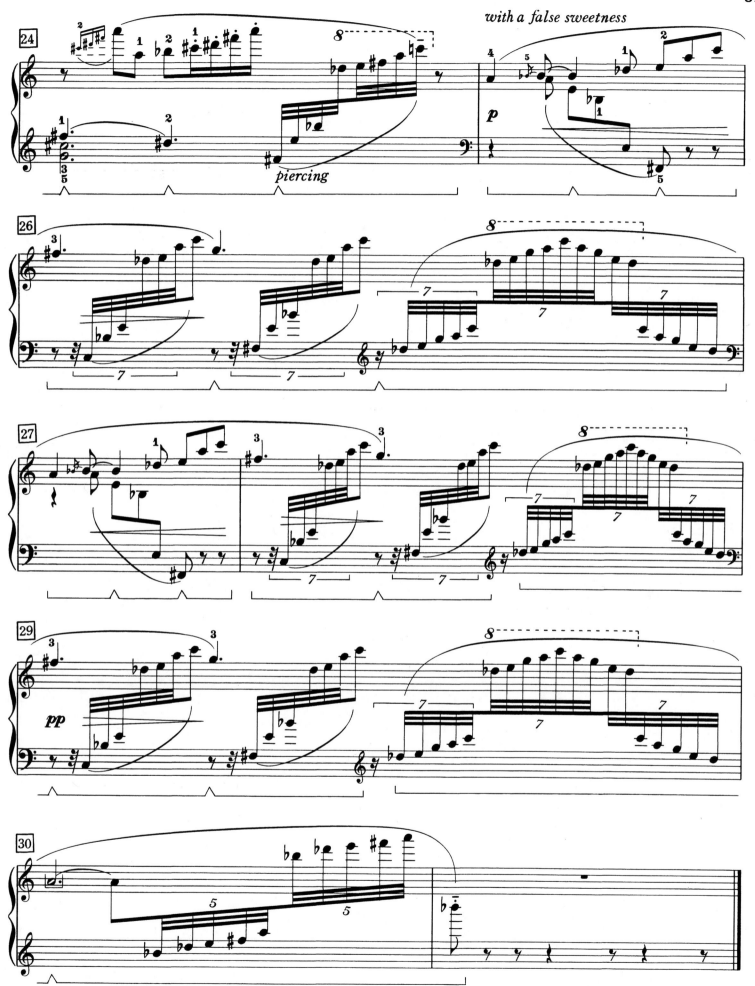

# Etude in Sevenths

Op. 65, No. 2
(1911 - 12)

# Etude in Fifths

Op. 65, No. 3
(1911 - 12)

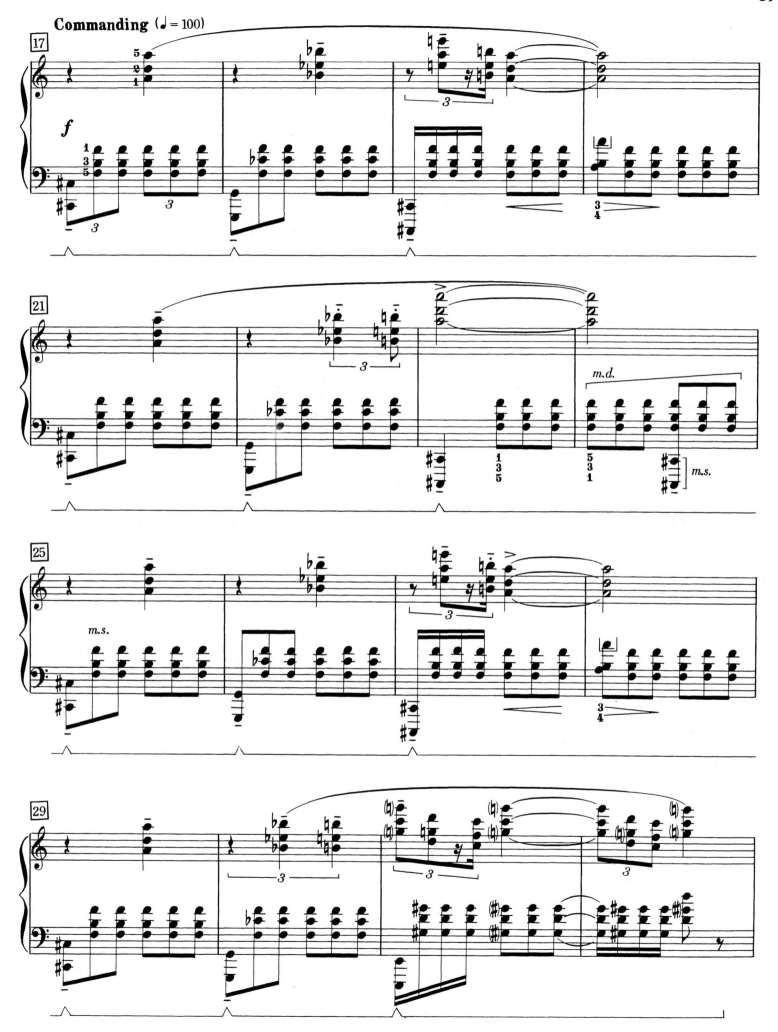

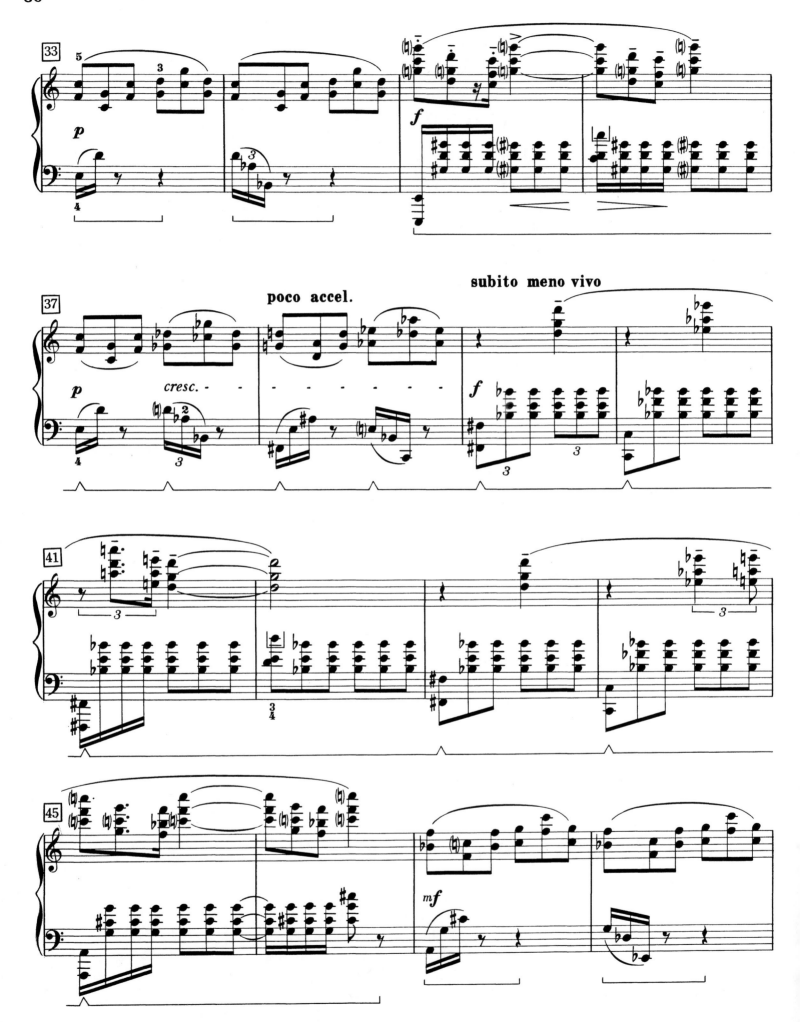

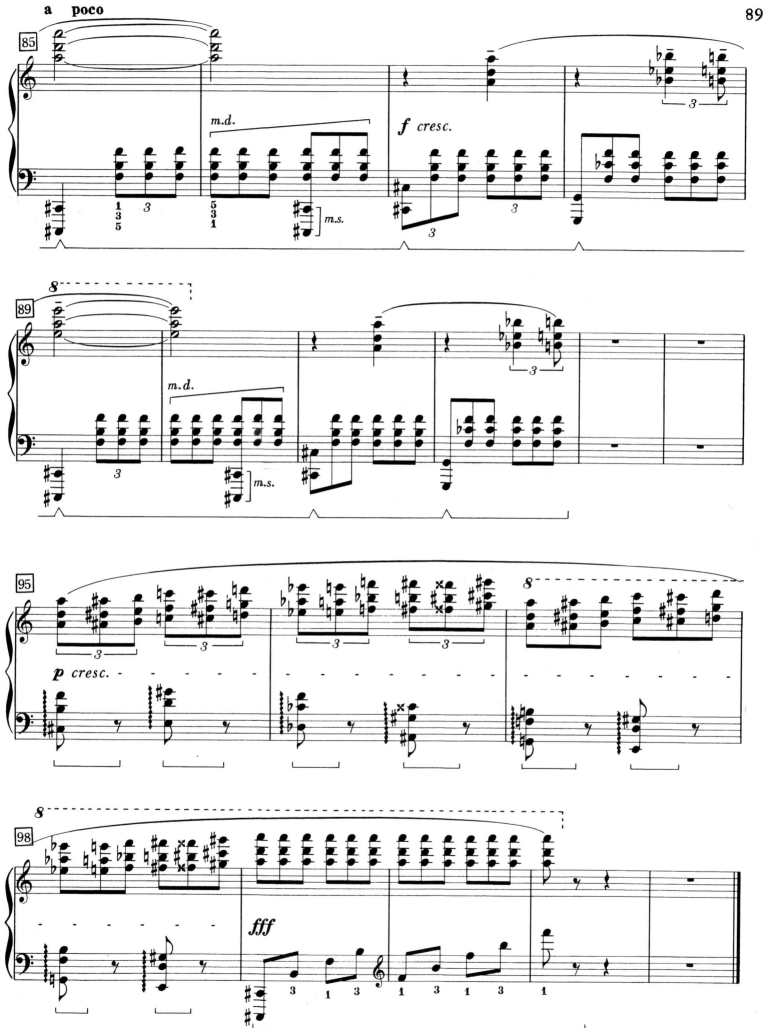

# Garlands
### (from Two Dances)

Op. 73, No. 1
(1914)

**With languorous grace** (♩ = C. 58)

# Prelude

Op.74, No.2
(1914)

**Very slow and meditative** ( ♪ = 66 )

* or try experimenting with the sostenuto !

# Prelude

Op.74, No.3
(1914)